Christmas
Spirit

Christmas
Spirit

Iris Howden

Published in association with
The Basic Skills Agency

Hodder & Stoughton
A MEMBER OF THE HODDER HEADLINE GROUP

Order queries: please contact Bookpoint Ltd, 39 Milton Park, Abingdon, Oxon
OX14 4TD. Telephone: (44) 01235 400414, Fax: (44) 1235 400454.
Lines are open from 9.00-6.00, Monday to Saturday, with a 24 hour message answering
service. Email address: orders@bookpoint.co.uk

British Library Cataloguing in Publication Data

Howden, Iris
    Christmas spirit. – (Chillers) (Livewire)
    1. Readers – English fiction
    I. Title   II. Basic Skills Agency
    428.6

ISBN 0 340 697571

First published 1997
Impression number   10 9 8 7 6 5 4
Year   2004 2003 2002 2001 2000 1999

Typeset by Fakenham Photosetting Ltd, Fakenham, Norfolk.
Printed in Great Britain for Hodder & Stoughton Educational,
a division of Hodder Headline Plc, 338 Euston Road, London NW1 3BH
by Athenæum Press Ltd, Gateshead, Tyne & Wear.

Christmas Spirit

Contents

1

Lost

Karl was lost.

He was in a hire car.

He had got it at the airport.

The map was not much good.

He should have bought a better one.

It showed only the main roads,

not the little lanes.

And the weather was bad.

It was snowing.

Soon it would be dark.

The airport had a hotel.

He should have spent the night there.

But he wanted to be home for Christmas.

He wanted to wake up at home.

He had been away in Hong Kong.

He had not seen his family for two years.

His mum and dad had moved house.

They had lived in a big town,

near their work.

When Karl and his sister left,

the house was too big for them.

'You'll love the cottage,' his mum wrote

in a letter.

'It is really pretty.

I've been working in the garden.

I can't wait for you to see it.'

He said the address out loud.

'Holly Cottage, Church Lane, Wetford.'

It sounded so English.

'It must be near a church', he thought.

Karl had missed England.

He had missed the weather.

He looked at the trees and fields.

They were white with snow,

just like a Christmas card. He liked that.

It was a change from Hong Kong.

It was hot and noisy there.

Hong Kong was full of people.

Everyone seemed busy.

They were always in a rush.

England was quiet.

He was looking forward to that.

He would enjoy being at home at last.

But he would have to hurry.

It would be dark soon.

And he did not know the way.

He wished he had a better map.

He saw two black crows ahead.

They were flying round and round.

2

Help At Hand

Karl looked for a sign post,

or someone to show him the way.

He saw a bridge up ahead.

There was a cottage next to it.

He would stop and ask there.

The crows had landed near the cottage.

Then he saw the woman.

She was up ahead by the road.

A woman in a dark cloak.

He had not seen her till just then.

That was strange.

She must have come out of the cottage.

The cottage looked dark.

There were no lights on.

The crows began to make a noise.

Karl drove up to the woman.

He stopped the car.

He wound down the window.

'Excuse me,' he said, 'Can you help me?

I'm looking for the village of Wetford.'

She turned her head slowly.

She was very pale.

Her eyes had dark rings round them,

but she was very pretty.

Karl saw she was just a young girl.

He said again, 'Can you help me?

I'm looking for the village of Wetford.'

He couldn't tell if she had heard.

He touched her arm.

It felt very cold.

His warm hand made her jump.

'You want the next road left,' she said.

She had a soft voice.

'I'm going there myself.'

'Get in,' Karl said.

'I'll give you a lift.'

3

Cold Air

He leaned over to open the door.

As she got in, a blast of cold air hit him.

The girl had a bunch of flowers.

They were white.

A sweet smell filled the car.

Karl drove on.

The girl did not speak.

She looked ahead into the dark.

The car felt colder and colder.

Her face and hands were as

white as the flowers.

Karl did all the talking.

He told her about Hong Kong.

He talked about his family.

He said he had missed them.

His sister had three children.

He had never seen her baby.

She had been born when

he was in Hong Kong.

They were coming for Christmas Day.

He had presents for them all.

'Hong Kong has some great shops,' he said.

'But it's good to be back.

To be home for Christmas.

I want to walk in the snow,

and be warm by the fire at night.'

Soon they came to the village.

'Where do you live?' Karl asked.

'Just drop me by the church,' she said.

'The lane you want is the next one.'

'I'll be here for a month,' Karl said.

'Perhaps we'll meet again.

My name's Karl. What's yours?'

'Laura,' said the girl, so softly

Karl could hardly hear the word.

She went quickly into the churchyard.

She pulled her cloak around her.

The two crows called to her.

They were sitting on a gravestone.

'What a strange girl,' Karl thought.

'She looked so pale and sad.

What was she doing out in the dark?'

He drove on. He was keen to get home.

The car felt warm again.

4

Home At Last

The cottage was just as he had hoped.

There was a Christmas tree in the window.

A log fire burned in the grate.

His mum made him sit down.

He needed to get warm.

She gave him some tea and a mince pie.

'It's lovely to see you, son,' she said.

'After all this time.

What do you think of the cottage?'

'It's great,' Karl told her.

'Just right for you and Dad.

It's not too big.

I can't wait to see it in the daylight.

What are the people like next door?'

'They are very nice,' his mum said.

'A young family live on one side.

An older lady lives on the other.

Poor woman. She lives all alone.

Her husband died years ago.

I must pop round and see her later.

It's a bad time of year for her.

Her daughter was killed on Christmas Eve.

It was three years ago today.

She was an only child.

She was a lovely girl too. Only 17.'

5

Hit-and-Run

'What happened to her?' Karl asked.

'She had gone to her grandmother's,'

his mum said. 'To take some flowers.

She lived in the cottage.

The one by the bridge.

Laura was hit by a car. A hit-and-run driver.

He never even stopped.

She died at once.

They never found the driver.'

'Did you say her name was Laura?' Karl asked.

He felt his skin go cold.

'Yes. It's a pretty name, isn't it?

Her grave is in the churchyard.

Her mother puts white flowers on it.

She visits the grave every day.

She always looks so sad.

Some say that she has a broken heart.

Two crows are always by the grave.

They seem to watch over it.

I'll show you later,' she said.

'Karl, it's so good to see you,' she went on.

'It's the best present a mother could wish for,

having her child home for Christmas.'

Karl went to the window.

He looked out into the darkness.

He could hear the two crows calling.

He felt cold.

'Goodnight, Laura,' he said softly.